21 Days

21 Days

From Fear to Faith

Rashon C Wallace

XULON PRESS

Xulon Press
2301 Lucien Way #415
Maitland, FL 32751
407.339.4217
www.xulonpress.com

© 2021 by Rashon C Wallace

All rights reserved solely by the author. The author guarantees all contents are original and do not infringe upon the legal rights of any other person or work. No part of this book may be reproduced in any form without the permission of the author.

Due to the changing nature of the Internet, if there are any web addresses, links, or URLs included in this manuscript, these may have been altered and may no longer be accessible. The views and opinions shared in this book belong solely to the author and do not necessarily reflect those of the publisher. The publisher therefore disclaims responsibility for the views or opinions expressed within the work.

Unless otherwise indicated, Scripture quotations taken from the King James Version (KJV)–*public domain.*

Scripture quotations taken from the Holy Bible, New International Version (NIV). Copyright © 1973, 1978, 1984, 2011 by Biblica, Inc.™. Used by permission. All rights reserved.

Scripture quotations taken from the Amplified Bible (AMP). Copyright © 1954, 1958, 1962, 1964, 1965, 1987 by The Lockman Foundation. Used by permission. All rights reserved.

Paperback ISBN-13: 978-1-66283-032-7
Ebook ISBN-13: 978-1-66283-033-4

Dedication

This book is dedicated to my mother, Lorraine D. Wallace, who from as early as I can remember taught me about Jesus. Due to her love for me I found abundant love from Him. I am grateful.

Introduction

Fear is a tool used by the enemy for your destruction. Fear is the enemy's number one weapon to keep you stuck and depressed. I am writing this book to remind you that although Satan is walking around like a lion seeking whom he can devour (1 Pet. 5:8), you have the power through the Holy Spirit to defeat him. The Bible reminds us that the weapons of our warfare are not carnal but mighty through God for the pulling down of strongholds (2 Cor. 10), which means we can fight back! That means Satan does not have to win the battle in your mind! That means we can conquer fear and doubt with the Word of God, with the Holy Spirit, through prayer!

In 1 Chronicles 28:20, King David told his son Solomon to be strong and courageous and to do the work. You see, God had already told King David that it would be Solomon who would build the temple. However, just because God made that declaration, it did not clear Solomon from having to do the work. My friend, Jesus came so that you can have life and have life more abundantly. That is a promise, but you have to do the work. To get what you paid for from this book, you have to do the work. Don't just read the pages—**live them** Make sure you say the declarations out loud each day several times per day. Make sure you read the verses from your Bible each day after you read the devotion. Do the work so that you can receive the promise.

Get ready, get set ... let's go, as you begin your 21-day journey from a life of fear to a life of faith!

Day 1

Now faith is the substance of things hoped for, the evidence of things not seen. — Hebrews 11:1 (KJV)

I know the next step that God wants me to take. I know what it is, but I don't know how in the world to do it, I am afraid. Can you relate to this? Since I was a little girl, I have loved school. So much so that when I was in kindergarten, I cried during the summer break because I wanted to go back to school. From the moment I found out what a doctoral degree was, I have wanted to pursue one. The application deadline for the program I want to apply to is one month from now. I feel like God keeps telling me to do it. I also feel like God has verified this through other sources as well, but in my mind, I keep telling myself, "How can I do it? I can't afford it, and I don't have time." I keep telling myself all the reasons why I shouldn't.

The Lord spoke to my heart very simply and said, "What is faith?" The Bible tells us in Hebrews 11:1 that "faith is the substance of things hoped for; it is the evidence of things not seen." I cannot see how God can do this; it seems impossible to me. But God told Abraham to "leave, go into the land that I will show you" (Gen. 12:1). God did not tell

Abraham exactly where to go. God did not tell Abraham how he was going to get there. God did not give Abraham a map; He just told him to go. I'm going to have to step out on faith, right? That application is due. I don't know, and I cannot see how it will happen, but I will believe God, and I will not be fearful. It seems impossible, but I am reminded of a quote from Nelson Mandela: "It always seems impossible until it's done." It seems impossible, but I am going to take a step of faith.

I recorded those words in a video on November 14, 2017. I am sitting in my office today, which is April 8, 2019, transcribing that spoken video into the written form of this book that you are reading right now. The thought of this brings tears to my eyes, not only because I am in school now, not only because I have taken several classes and currently have a 3.8 GPA, and not only because within that time, I also became a licensed minister. I have tears in my eyes because right now, at this time, despite all those accomplishments, I still feel fearful. God told me to write this book, and I don't have time to write it. God told me to write this book, and I don't know the first thing about publishing a book. I have tears in my eyes because I know that if God was faithful to me on November 14, 2017, He will continue to be faithful to me. I am fearful because I cannot see how this book will get published, but I believe it will. I am tearful because it always seems impossible until it's done.

I don't know what I am doing; I plan to simply trust God. I pray that will be your plan as well. And as you hold this book in your hands, know this: the woman who wrote it was terrified, not capable, not well connected, not great. However remember that God uses the foolish things of this world to confound the wise. If God can do it for me, He can do it for you too. Whatever God put on your heart to do, start it today! Write that book. Start that blog. Have that baby. Go back to school. Open that business. I dare you to believe God for the impossible.

As you can see below, there will be verbal declarations and a Bible reading for each day of this journey. Read the Bible passage and take the time to think about it. Repeat the daily affirmations to yourself out loud! Yes, I meant out loud. Throughout the day today, as you hear those voices of fear in your head, cast them out with these words. Don't be afraid to do this! It is a necessary part of this journey.

Today's Declaration:

"I dare to believe God for the impossible."

Today's Bible Reading:

Hebrews 11:1–6

Genesis 12:1–4

Today's Prayer

Dear Lord,

I do not know what I am doing. I trust You with my whole life. I pray in the name of Jesus that You will release me from fear and that You will remind me that all things are possible when I lean in and trust You. Father God, thank you for being my strength. Thank you for being my courage. I humbly submit my life to You, and I believe You for great things. In Jesus's name, I pray. Amen.

Day 2

May your choices reflect your hopes and not your fears. — Nelson Mandela

My friend, my hope for you today and from this day forward is that your choices will begin to reflect your hopes and not your fears. Each day we are tempted to make choices based on our fears; if you decided to pick up this book, it is clear that you don't want fear controlling your life anymore. In the Bible, there is a story of two women, Mary and Martha. In this story, Martha allowed the anxieties of life (her fears) to take her focus away from Jesus. The story is found in Luke 10:38–42; the ESV version says:

> As Jesus and his disciples were on their way, he came to a village where a woman named Martha opened her home to him. She had a sister called Mary, who sat at the Lord's feet, listening to what he said. But Martha was distracted by all the preparations that had to be made. She came to him and asked, "Lord, don't you care that my sister has left me to do the work by myself? Tell her to help me!" "Martha, Martha,"

> the Lord answered, "you are worried and upset about many things, but few things are needed—or indeed only one. Mary has chosen what is better, and it will not be taken away from her."

You see, Mary chose to take her time and spend it with Jesus, while Martha spent her time worrying (that is, being anxious and fearful). I can imagine that Martha was afraid her house or dinner was not going to be just right or nervous that Mary was getting to spend more time with Jesus than she was able to because of her preparations.

Before writing this book, I identified with Martha (actually, sometimes I still do); I can be careful, worried, and anxious about many things. If I am honest, I can admit that some of my fears are related to underestimating God's willingness to provide for me. I have wondered why God would want to take care of someone like me. I have messed up many times, made terrible choices, and have not lived up to who God has called me to be. I know that God is all-powerful, faithful, and loving. However, there have been times in my life when I have doubted that I was deserving. Somewhere between believing God, reading my Bible, and attending church, I forgot that God could and would provide for me despite my shortcomings, sins, and even occasional unbelief.

As we begin this journey, you may feel like Martha. You may be anxious and worried about many things. You may feel like I have in the past—undeserving of God's love and mercy. God does not want you to live that way anymore. Begin to meditate on Nelson Mandela's quote from the beginning of this chapter and allow it to become your way of life. Allow your life choices to reflect your hopes and not your fears.

Today's Declarations:

"I make choices based on hope and not fear."

"God loves me despite my flaws."

Today's Bible Reading:

Luke 10:38–42 (reread this and ask God to speak to you)

Today's Prayer:

Father God,
  Thank you for another day. God, please remove fear, doubt, and anxiety from my heart and mind. Please remind me that You love me and have a good plan for my life. Father God, in the name of Jesus, please allow every single choice I make today to be based on the hope I have in You. In the precious name of Jesus, I pray. Amen.

Day 3

When he heard this, Jesus said, "This sickness will not end in death. No, it is for God's glory so that God's Son may be glorified through it."
— John 11:4 (NIV)

I'm not sure what your sickness is. You may have an actual illness in your body; you may have a broken heart, a broken relationship, a tremendous worry or fear. I don't know what is troubling you, but I know that Satan will try to use whatever it is to make you feel like death, to make you feel like you will never overcome it. Today's scripture reminds us that God can bring dead things back to life, even in the most terrible situations. Do you remember Mary and Martha from yesterday's story? Well, in today's reading, Mary and Martha's brother Lazarus is sick. Jesus tells them not to worry, that his sickness will bring God glory, *and* then Lazarus dies! Like, for real? But listen, Jesus brings Lazarus back to life, and God got the glory! You see, the thing that feels like death in your life can become new again. We serve a God who has a track record for bringing dead things back to life. Jesus brought Lazarus back to life. Jesus came back to life after dying on the cross, and the situation in your life can come back to life as well.

My son was born with a serious disease. When he was just a few hours old, we knew that something was wrong. Due to his sickness, we had to leave the hospital where I gave birth to him and take an ambulance to the children's hospital in our city. He had to have major surgery when he was just three months old and was in and out of the hospital for the first five years of his life. As a result of my son's illness, I fell into a deep depression and experienced a significant amount of anxiety. It was one of the darkest moments in my life.

Due to my depression, there were days when I could not even get out of bed. I knew I needed help. So, I scheduled an appointment with a Christian psychologist. This psychologist helped me learn to calm my anxiety and fear with the Word of God. He shared with me the importance of memorizing scripture to help guide me through difficult times. One of the scriptures that he used with me was Psalm 23. He had me repeat Psalm 23 when I was anxious, worried, or feeling depressed. There were many nights when Psalm 23 helped me fall asleep, and it was Psalm 23 that kept me going throughout most days. The psychologist told me to visualize the words of the psalm in my head. I am going to ask you to do that with me today. If you have access to an audio version of the Bible, please listen to Psalm 23 now. If not please read it aloud to yourself. Close your eyes, listen, and see the imagery that the scripture creates in your mind. (Listen before you move on.)

Psalm 23 tells us that the Lord is our shepherd. He leads us beside the still waters; He restores our souls; He makes us lie down in green pastures. If you can see that in your mind's eye and you can see the healing, rest, and peace that become apparent with those images, you can see that God can give us peace, rest, and healing if we allow ourselves to rest in Him.

The metaphor of God as our shepherd is one of the most closely held images in the Bible. A good shepherd feeds his lambs and goats and gives them fresh water. A good shepherd grooms his sheep, delivers new baby lambs, and directs his sheep to stay together for safety and unity. A shepherd's job is to seek after any lost sheep. This is what God does for his children, and that is why we call Him our shepherd.

Sometimes we may find ourselves saying things like, "I need to pay this bill," "I want a new car," or "I need a new job." What usually happens is that we begin to worry because the thing that we want or need is not happening as fast as we would like it to. When we don't get the job, when we don't have the money, when the healing has not come, we begin to grow more and more afraid because we are worried about what we will do if it does not happen. **I want to assure you today that God knows exactly what you need**. The part of Psalm 23 that says "thou shall not want" means *you are okay*. You don't have to want because your shepherd, the Lord, knows what you need. That means God will supply everything you need in His time. That's the hard part—in His time. I know for sure that everything has a beginning, a middle, and an end. I also know that the middle is the hardest part. So, if you are in that middle part today, hold on! The end is coming. In the meantime, it's okay to lie down in green pastures. It is okay to walk beside those still waters and allow God to restore your soul.

I want to let you know that my son had his surgery sixteen years ago. He has not been hospitalized in over ten years, and at our last specialist appointment, the doctor said he was doing excellent and couldn't be doing any better! Sixteen years ago, I thought my son was going to die. To be honest, some days, I thought I was going to die from the stress of it all. However, God is a healer, and He is faithful. My son's sickness was not to his death but to God's glory. Today, my friend, I need you to believe that the "thing" will not kill you. That you will live, and God will get the glory. I pray that you will not be afraid today. God is right by your side. God is making a way.

Today's Declarations: (say these things out loud; scream them if you have to)

"The Lord takes care of all of my needs."

"I am okay!"

Today's Bible Reading:

John 11:1–44

Today's Prayer:

Dear Lord,

Thank you for being the Lord of new beginnings. Thank you for being the Lord who makes dead things live. I pray in the name of Jesus that You will make the old things new in my life. Lord, please continue to heal the broken things in my life. Please continue to heal the sickness, the worry, the disease. Please heal my mind so that I can see how big and how wide Your love is for me. I love you, Lord, and ask all these blessings in Jesus's name. Amen.

Day 4

The Lord is my shepherd; I shall not want. He maketh me to lie down in green pastures: he leadeth me beside the still waters. He restoreth my soul: he leadeth me in the paths of righteousness for his name's sake. Yea, though I walk through the valley of the shadow of death, I will fear no evil: for thou art with me; thy rod and thy staff they comfort me. Thou preparest a table before me in the presence of mine enemies: thou anointest my head with oil; my cup runneth over. Surely goodness and mercy shall follow me all the days of my life: and I will dwell in the house of the Lord forever. — Psalm 23

Since the Lord is our shepherd, that means we are His sheep. Do you know about sheep? Sheep have a tough time doing anything alone. They always travel in packs. If one sheep gets away from the group, he will be lost! And let's not even talk about if a sheep happens to get turned over onto its back! Search online for a sheep who is turned on its back. It is practically impossible for them to get back on their feet by themselves; it takes them forever! It is no coincidence that God likens us to sheep. When we get turned upside down, we need the shepherd's help to get us back on our feet. We cannot do it alone.

There are different stages in Psalm 23, kind of like the stages of life. Let's talk about the stage of the valley and the shadow of death—you know, that dark place that we have all experienced at some point in our lives, the place that people don't like to talk about. The text says that there is a *shadow* of death. For some of you reading this today, your life may feel dark. You may feel like you will never get out of this place. Well, I am here to tell you that it is just a shadow! Yes, you may be in a valley because, in life, we all have valleys, hills, highs, and lows that are all part of the terrain. Today, if you feel like you are in that valley of the shadow of death, let me encourage you. Remember that death has not come upon you; it is just a shadow. Don't be afraid of your own shadow! Keep going because it is the responsibility of your shepherd, the Lord, to take care of you and bring you out of it.

Psalm 23 also talks about God's rod and staff. In biblical times, a shepherd was generally equipped with both a staff and a rod. The rod was a two- to four-foot club used for defending the sheep from predators and robbers. The staff was used to keep sheep from wandering off. The staff had a curved end that fit the sheep's neck perfectly so that the shepherd could pull and correct the sheep to help them stay on course. So it is with you, my friend; we all need correction, discipline, and even disappointment for us to stay on the right path in our life. It is not a good feeling, but it is necessary. God will use His rod to protect us from danger and keep us on the right path, to keep us from wandering off and getting turned on our backs.

Can I encourage you today? If you feel like you are in a place where the shadow of death is upon you and you are being hit by the shepherd's rod, remember that your shepherd will keep you under his care. Don't give up now. The psalm goes on to say that God will anoint your head with oil. Why the oil? When a fly lands on a sheep's nose, it will often travel up the nose and lay eggs, which turn into worms that can burrow into the brain. As a result, the sheep will bang its head, trying to get rid of the irritation. The sheep can die from this. So, every day the shepherd pours oil on the sheep's nose, and the flies slide out instead of flying into and irritating the sheep's brain. You see, we can come to God, and He can anoint us with oil that will allow the irritants in our minds and our lives to be removed. Hallelujah! Allow God to anoint your head with oil so that your cup runs over. Allow His goodness and mercy to follow you all the days of your life. Allow that goodness and mercy to follow you today. God bless you. Have a wonderful day!

Today's Declarations:

"God's goodness and mercy follow me today and every day!"
"I will not be afraid of the **shadow** of death."

"My head is anointed with oil, and outside irritants don't bother my mind."

Today's Bible Reading:

Psalm 23

Today's Prayer

Dear Father God,

There are people who are reading this book today who feel like they are walking in the shadow of death. There are people who are reading this book today who feel like all hope is lost. I pray that You will sit next to them today. I pray that You will sit next to them right now. I pray that they will feel Your presence as they read these words. Father God, I pray that You will be the lifter of their head. I pray that You will shepherd them with Your loving arms and will hide them under Your wing, where they can find rest, peace, and joy. You are our Father, and we trust You. We ask all these blessings in Jesus's name. Amen.

Day 5

Even though I walk through the darkest valley, I will fear no evil, — Psalm 23:4

Yesterday, after I posted my video blog on Facebook, I had several people reach out to me. I spoke about how scary it has been for me to post such personal messages about my life and relationship with God and how vulnerable I felt. A friend encouraged me to keep posting the videos. I said to her, "I don't know what I am doing." The truth is, I am working through life and doing the best that I can, but most of the time, I am scared and confused. She responded: "Do it afraid!" So that is our mantra for today—do it afraid! Whatever God has put in your heart, I challenge you to do it. I challenge you to do it **today**. I challenge you to do it even if you are afraid!

If we go back into Psalm 23, the idea of doing it afraid remains relevant. Fear can sometimes paralyze us. It can make us afraid to move, and as a result, we simply remain still. We become beautiful, God-fearing, church-attending statues. We remain trapped in the circumstances and in a life we do not want. Some of us have stayed in the same place for months. Some of us have remained in the same place for years.

In Psalm 23, verse 3, the writer says: "He restoreth my soul: he leadeth me in the paths of righteousness for his name's sake." If God is leading you in paths of righteousness for His name's sake, that means you are moving! That means you are not stuck. Stop being stuck! Allow God to lead you on a path of righteousness for His name's sake. God is leading you; are you listening? God is speaking to you; can you hear Him? As a shepherd, it is God's job to guide and protect us. God can lead in a variety of ways. God may lead you through a spoken word, through the written Word in the scriptures, or through an experience or a circumstance.

I believe if you are reading this book, it is not an accident. God is speaking to your heart about something. I believe God is leading you on that path of righteousness. Are you going to go, or will you remain stuck in fear? For you to hear how God is leading you, you have to be close to Him. You have to be still in God. You also have to read and know His Word. If you are not actively reading the Word, it will be hard to know for sure where God is leading you.

I encourage you today to keep going. As God's sheep, we hear His voice (John 10:27). If God has spoken to you about something that He wants you to do, do it! If you cannot hear God's voice, it doesn't mean you are not one of His sheep. It may mean you are not listening or not praying or not reading the Word. If you cannot hear His voice in a particular area, slow down a bit. Quiet yourself and rest in God. Sometimes you just need to be still so you can hear God talking. You need to climb into scripture so through

God's written Word, you can hear what He says to you. I encourage you to keep going today. Allow God to lead you on a path of righteousness for His namesake.

Today's Declarations:

"Do it afraid."

Today's Bible Reading:

John 10:1–16

Today's Prayer

Father God, I thank you for this Word today. I thank you for this revelation that I can walk with You and I don't have to be stuck anymore. I pray that You will help me to move, that You will allow me to walk today, that You will help me to remember that You are right by my side. I thank you in advance for the mighty move of God that is happening in my life right now. I thank you for the shift in direction, I thank you for the new thing that is happening in my life. I ask all these blessings in Jesus's name. Amen.

Day 6

You desire but do not have, so you kill. You covet, but you cannot get what you want, so you quarrel and fight. You do not have because you do not ask God. — James 4:2 (NIV)

Wow! **You** do not have because **you** do not ask. Sometimes we don't ask for things because we are paralyzed with fear. We can be so scared that we don't even think of asking God for what we need. I have been in that situation before. A few days after the birth of my daughter, I developed the worst headache of my life. I called the doctor and she had me come into the office. The doctor told me I was experiencing a reaction to the epidural and gave me pain medication. I went home and stayed home for a day or two with this horrible headache. One evening, my sister got off work and drove to my house. When she arrived, she told me I had to go to the hospital. I thank God for my sister doing that because she saved my life. When I arrived at the hospital, they discovered that a blood clot had developed in my brain. I was then rushed by ambulance to a different hospital, which specialized in stroke care.

Once at the second hospital, I was put into the intensive care unit. I stayed in intensive care for a few days and then was put into the main hospital for about two weeks. I cannot remember a lot from that time, but I remember I was in tremendous pain, and I was very, very scared. I thought I was going to die. I felt I was never going to see my daughter or my son again. I also thought they would shave all my hair off and cut my skull open to remove the clot (which did not happen). Pretty much, my fears were death and a shaved head, and at that time, both of those options felt scary!

I had a friend who has since passed away; her name was April. April was a wonderful woman of God. April was intelligent and wise beyond her years. Once April found out I was in the hospital, she visited me every day (she worked as a therapist in the hospital). One day when April came, I was crying, and she asked me what I wanted God to do for me. At that point, the only thing I could think of was that I wanted to see my baby girl. My daughter could not come to the hospital because she was just a few weeks old and had not had her shots yet. April said to me very simply, "We will pray today that you will be able to go home tomorrow." April prayed, and she put Post-it Notes all over my hospital room. I even had Post-it Notes on my IV pole! Throughout that day, between the pain, I meditated on the scriptures she had posted in the room. I believed what April said, though I had not dared to ask for it myself.

The next day a new doctor was assigned to my case, and she said I could go home! All the other doctors who had been working with me would not allow me to leave. God put a new doctor in charge, who let me go home so I could see my newborn daughter. The point of this story is that I was afraid to ask God for what I wanted. I thank God for my friend, who was not afraid to ask God for what I wanted. I don't know what you need, but I am telling you today to get on your knees and ask God for it. Prayer is our most effective weapon against fear. Get on your knees and ask God today for the thing that you need. I pray that you will continue to read the Word of God and that His word will saturate your mind and your spirit.

Today's Declaration

"I am not afraid to ask God for what I need."

"God will hear and answer my prayer."

Today's Bible Reading:

James 4:1–10

Today's Prayer

Dear Lord,

Thank you for reminding me today that I have not because I ask not. Please give me the courage today to ask for my dreams. Please give me the courage today to ask for my wants. God, help me to pour out my requests humbly and with thanksgiving. I thank you in advance for what You are doing and what You will do, and I believe that my eyes have not seen, that my ears have not heard, and that I can't even imagine all the good things that You have in store for me because I love you. I praise you, Father God. I ask all these blessings in Jesus's name. Amen.

Day 7

This is the confidence we have in approaching God: that if we ask anything according to his will, he hears us. And if we know that he hears us-whatever we ask-we know that we have what we asked him. — 1 John 5:14–15 (NIV)

Yesterday we talked about how prayer is our most effective weapon against fear. Paul tells us in 1 Thessalonians 5:17 to pray without ceasing. That means to pray all the time. Pray while you are driving, while in the shower, while eating, pray while working. **Pray all of the time.** So, let's do that today.

Heavenly Father, we come to You, giving You all the praise, all the honor, and all the glory. Recognizing that You are a good God, You are a gracious God, and You are a kind God. We stand before You today with needs. Some of us have many fears. However, we know that You are God. We know that You are the **Great I Am.** *We know that we can come to You with a humble heart and ask and that You will hear and answer us. We know that You are a just God. We know that if we ask anything that is in line with Your will, You will do it! We ask You today, Lord, to please remove fear from our lives.*

We know that Your Word says that You have not given us the spirit of fear but of power, love, and a sound mind. Right now, in the name of Jesus, I pray that every person who reads this prayer will walk in faith and with confidence in their lives. I pray that You release the spirit of fear from them. I pray that fear will be replaced with power, love, and soundness of mind in the name of Jesus. Your Word tells us that if my people who are called by my name would humble themselves and pray and seek Your face and turn from their wicked ways then You will hear from heaven, forgive sin, and heal the land. I pray that right now, in the name of Jesus, You will heal the lives of the people who are reading this prayer. Please, Father God, heal hearts and minds and households. I pray that You restore our souls. Father God, please walk into our hearts and minds and do what Your Word promises. Please lift heavy spirits and release burdens today in Jesus's name. Help us to reach for You today and every day. Help us to be steadfast in prayer today and every day. Help us to read and meditate on Your Word today and every day. In Jesus's name, we pray. Amen.

Today's Declarations:

"I pray without ceasing."

"God hears and answers my prayers."

Today's Bible Reading:

I Thessalonians 5:16–18
I John 5:14–15

Day 8

Build a wall of scriptures around you, and you will see that the world cannot break it down. — Ellen Gould White

There are two scriptures that I am going to ask you to memorize. You can put these scriptures on a sticky note and stick them to your mirror, your computer, and the dashboard of your car. I used to stick Bible verses on the cabinets in my kitchen (since I was there so much cooking and washing dishes!). Put these sticky notes wherever you spend time. Allow these scriptures to become a part of who you are, a part of your thinking and being. The verses are:

2 Timothy 1:7 (KJV)

> For God hath not given us the spirit of fear, but of power, and of love, and of a sound mind.

Psalm 27:13 (KJV)

> I had fainted unless I had believed to see the goodness of the Lord in the land of the living.

The books of first and second Timothy are written by the Apostle Paul. 2 Timothy is one of Paul's last letters. When Paul wrote this letter, it was a personal letter meant to encourage Timothy. Timothy was younger than Paul and just starting in ministry. Paul wanted to give wisdom regarding how to live a Christian life and lead people in their faith walk. Paul told Timothy that God has not given us the spirit of fear but of power, of love, and a sound mind. Let me repeat that, **God has not given you a spirit of fear but of power, love and a sound mind!** If you are feeling fearful, know that that does not come from God. The amplified Bible says it this way:

2 Timothy 1:7 (AMPC)

> For God did not give us a spirit of timidity (of cowardice, of craven and cringing and fawning fear), but [He has given us a spirit] of power and of love and of calm *and* well-balanced mind *and* discipline *and* self-control.

Power is aggressive energy in the face of difficulty, which overcomes weakness and enables one to work and to endure. God gives us power! God gives us aggressive energy in the face of difficulty that will indeed enable us to work through those difficulties that we face in life. Sometimes we don't feel like we have any power. If you have felt that way, you are not alone. That feeling is a trick of the enemy. Satan wants you to feel like you are alone, like you are the only person in the world who is experiencing this problem.

I was talking to a friend the other day, and I was sharing a difficulty that I am experiencing in my life right now. I am facing this thing that makes me feel embarrassed, and it is something that I typically do not share with others. Once I told her about it, she said to me, "Wow, I did not know that. I am dealing with a very similar issue." My friend and I started talking about ideas and things we could do to tackle this problem and ways we could help ourselves and each other. As we were getting off the phone, she said to me, "I am so encouraged because I don't feel alone anymore."

Whatever you are experiencing today, trust me when I say **you are not alone**! Very often, we don't talk about our pain and hardships. We put on a mask to appear perfect (especially on social media). We are all dealing with life's issues and demands. That brings me to one of my favorite scriptures, which is found in Psalm 27:13. "I had fainted unless I had believed to see the goodness of the Lord in the land of the living." King David wrote that. He said he would have fainted, he would have given up, he would not have been able to go on unless he believed he would see the goodness of God right here on earth. Goodness and blessings from God are not something we have to wait for until we get to heaven. They are things we have faith for and can receive now, right here in our towns, on our streets, in our homes, and in our lives.

I pray that you can hold on to those verses today and remember and believe that God has given you the power to stand up in the face of whatever you are experiencing in your life. I pray that you will walk in that power today. I pray that you will memorize these verses and repeat them over and over in your mind.

Today's Declarations:

"God has not given me the spirit of fear, but of power, love, and a sound mind."

"I will not faint; I believe that I will see God's goodness in my life."

Today's Bible Reading:

Psalm 27:1–14

Today's Prayer

Dear Father God,

Thank you for another day in the land of the living. I pray that You will empower me with Your strength and love. Father God, I can do nothing on my own, but I know that with You, everything is possible, so I pray that You take away the spirit of fear and help me to walk boldly into the destiny You have created for me. In Jesus's name, I pray. Amen.

Day 9

There are only two emotions in the world: love and fear. — Elisabeth Kübler-Ross

Yesterday I asked you to memorize 2 Timothy 1:7 (KJV). It says: "For God hath not given us the spirit of fear, but of power, and of love, and of a sound mind." If God did not give us fear, what did He give us? He gave us power, His perfect love, and the ability to have a sound and healthy mind.

I believe that love and fear are cousins. Cousins, that's right! You know how you have some cousins you love and you look forward to spending time with? Then you have those cousins who you rarely see, don't really like spending time with, but are connected to them simply because of your blood relation? I say love and fear are cousins because they are related to each other, but they just don't like to hang out together! Everything you do comes from either a place of love or a place of fear. When we are afraid, we act out negative things like anger, jealousy, and negative emotions. When we love, we act out patience and kindness and positive emotions. I cannot talk about love without thinking about the love chapter in 1 Corinthians 13:4–8 (NIV).

> Love is patient; love is kind. It does not envy; it does not boast; it is not proud. It does not dishonor others; it is not self-seeking; it is not easily angered; it keeps no record of wrongs. Love does not delight in evil but rejoices with the truth. It always protects, always trusts, always hopes, always perseveres. Love never fails

This scripture tells us what love is. Love is not just a feeling. Love is an action. As Christians, we must walk in love. The greatest commandment is to love God with all your heart, mind, and soul, and to love others as yourself (Matt. 22:35–40). If you are fearful about doing something that God has called you to do, it could be because you do not adequately love yourself. I know that is a hard pill to swallow. It is important to love others, but we also have to love ourselves. As we look at this scripture and see love being described, let's relate that to ourselves. Love is patient. Are you patient with yourself? If you are trying something new, you will have setbacks; you will make mistakes. Since we are made from dust, we make mistakes every single day. If you are doing something new and it does not work out, it's okay! Try it again or try it a different way. Be patient with yourself!

Love is kind. Are you kind to yourself? We all have things we say to ourselves in our heads. They are like scripts we tell ourselves over and over. We say things like, "I'm not pretty enough," or "I'm not smart enough," or "I'm not successful enough," or "I can't do anything right." All of us say things like that to ourselves from time to time. However, if these are thoughts you think consistently, you are not kind to yourself. How do we fight against thoughts like those? One way is to memorize scripture so that when those negative thoughts come into your mind, you can fight back with the Word of God. To fight those harmful scripts you play in your head, remember that love is kind and that kindness should be shown to others and yourself.

The love chapter says that love does not envy. Be careful because when you are fearful, it is easy to become envious of things you don't have. It is easy to look at other people and say, "Why do they have that, and I don't?" "Why are they so pretty?" "Why are they so successful?" What we know is that God has given each one of us a gift. It says in 1 Corinthians 12:4–11 (NIV):

> There are different kinds of gifts, but the same spirit distributes them. There are different kinds of service, but the same Lord. There are different kinds of working, but in all of them and in everyone it is the same God at work.

Your gift will not be the same as someone else's. If you have not found out what your gift is, you should pray about it. One way to tell your gift is to look at what you are good at. Think about what gives you joy when you do it. Look at what you do that comes very naturally to you. Focusing on these things can begin to lead you to what your spiritual gift may be.

Love does not dishonor others, and it is not self-seeking; it is not easily angered. Sometimes we can be so fearful of things or challenging circumstances that we feel those circumstances will overtake us. As a result, we walk in fear, but it presents itself to others as anger. For example, someone cuts you off while driving, and you are ready to stick up your middle finger. Or someone says something to you that you don't like and you cuss them out. Whatever is in your heart comes out of your mouth. Today, let's focus on love. Let's focus on loving others and loving ourselves. Love yourself enough today to recognize that there are no barriers to the love, hope, and joy God has for you. Release yourself from the fear in your mind and live the life you were destined to live. Embrace love today toward yourself and others! Have a wonderful day.

Today's Declaration:

"I walk in love."
"I am patient and kind to myself and others."

Today's Bible Reading:

1 Corinthians 12:1–31

1 Corinthians 13:1–13

Today's Prayer

Father God,

I pray that You will strengthen me to walk in love toward others, to love myself, and to love You with all my heart, mind, and soul. Please help me to remember that love is patient, that love is kind, and that love keeps no record of wrongdoing. Please help me to be gentle with myself and gentle with others. Lord, thank you for another day. In Jesus's name, I pray. Amen.

Day 10

If you want to tap into what life has to offer, let love be your primary mode of being, not fear. — John Mark Green

Yesterday we talked about love and how you can either walk in fear or love. In 1 Corinthians 13:4–8, we are told that love is patient and kind, that love does not envy, boast, and is not proud. It further states that love does not dishonor others; it is not self-seeking, is not easily angered, and keeps no record of wrongs. Love does not delight in evil but rejoices with the truth. Lastly, love always protects, always trusts, always hopes, always perseveres, and never fails.

You are much more likely to display things like anger, bitterness, and selfish ambition when you walk in fear. Some of the most horrible things I have said and done have come out of places of fear. An example of that is when I went through a divorce. I was angry, scared, and exhibited behavior I am ashamed of. At that time, my biggest fear was being alone for the rest of my life. I was also afraid of what was going to happen to my children due to the divorce. If I peeled that back even further, I was afraid of being a "bad" mother and of what other people would think of me. Lastly, I was afraid of the financial pressure of it all. How was I going to be able to afford to give my kids everything they wanted and needed? As a result of walking around with all of that fear for the next few years, I made terrible choices. I thank God for forgiveness. I thank God for his mercy and grace. I thank God for not giving up on me. Praise God! I look back on that time in my life and can genuinely say that I learned from it.

I learned that when I am experiencing negative emotions (anger, disappointment, frustration), I have to peel it back and ask myself, "What are you afraid of?" That is what I am going to ask you to do today. Whatever emotions you are experiencing right now, take a moment to peel it back. Peel back your anger, your rage, your sadness, your disappointment. Ask yourself, "What am I afraid of?" When the answer comes to you, pray about it. Remember, 1 Timothy 1:7, God has not given us a spirit of fear but of power, love, and a sound mind. Once you discover what you are afraid of, approach that fear with the principles of love. Approach that fear with patience, kindness, without envy, without behaving rudely, without being self-seeking. Approach that fear with hope and perseverance and remember that love never fails. That is, no matter how the situation works out, love will win, even if it does not look like it. That means even if the situation does not work out the way you want it to, love wins because your heart will grow, your strength will increase, and your courage will develop.

Experiencing a divorce did not feel like a win. It was full of pain and sadness for myself, my children, my former husband, and even our extended family and friends. However, love allowed me to learn from the experience. The ability to love myself allowed me to change how I react to negative circumstances. Even though it was challenging, self-love allowed me to gain something from it. Today, I ask you to look at your challenging experiences, bad choices, and mistakes. Have the courage to look at them from the lens of love (for yourself). Ask yourself these questions:

- What did I learn?
- What can I gain from that experience?
- What did the experience teach me about loving myself?
- What did the experience teach me about loving others?

Take some time to reflect on these questions today. Carve out a quiet space, maybe grab a notebook or your computer and write down these questions and your answers. Take some time to think and pray. This will not be easy, but I encourage you to do the work, my friend. May God bless you, may God keep you, may his face shine upon you. Have a wonderful day!

Today's Declaration:

"I will not allow fear to make me bitter, selfish, or rude."
"I love myself."

Today's Bible Reading:

I Corinthians 13:1–13 (yep, reread it!)

Today's Prayer

Dear Lord,

Please allow me today to learn from my experiences. Please help me to take the things I have experienced and get something positive from them. Please help me to be gentle with those memories and be gentle with myself. Father God, please remind me today that You have not given me a spirit of fear but of power, love, and a sound mind. Please help me to walk in that soundness of mind today. Help me walk in that love today. In Jesus's name, I pray. Amen.

Day 11

I am the vine; you are the branches. If you remain in me and I in you, you will bear much fruit; apart from me, you can do nothing. — John 15:5

One of the biggest mistakes we can make as Christians is to believe we can do anything good on our own. We can do nothing without the power and the aid of the Holy Spirit in our lives. One reason life is challenging is because we try to do things in our own strength. Let me be very clear—if you could have done it by yourself, you would have done it by now! We need power from God to do everything in our lives. Will you please take a moment now to stop and think about all the things God has allowed you to accomplish and overcome in your life? Now say, "Thank you, God!"

Paul tells us in 2 Corinthians 12:9 that through our weakness, God is made strong. John 15:5 says we can do nothing apart from God. As you take this journey from fear to faith, it is essential to realize you cannot do it on your own. You will fail. Ask God for His power; ask God to help you walk in love. Ask God to release you from fear and doubt. Ask God to do a new thing in you. Ask God to help you to see yourself the way that He sees you. Please spend the next few moments in prayer. I ask that you pour your heart out to the Lord and ask Him for His help. Next, sit quietly for some time. Close your eyes and be still. Allow God to speak to your heart.

The Word of God is powerful; **it is alive** and active. It is sharper than any double-edged sword; it penetrates even to dividing soul and spirit, joints, and marrow. (Heb. 4:12). The Word of God tells us in Philippians 4:13 that we can do all things through Christ who gives us strength. Remember as you walk through your day today that you have no power of your own, that you have no strength of your own. Today, acknowledge that your strength comes from dependency on God. Remember that it is okay to be weak. The book of Matthew 11:28–30(NIV) says this:

> "Come to me, all you who are weary and burdened, and I will give you rest. Take my yoke upon you and learn from me, for I am gentle and humble in heart, and you will find rest for your souls. For my yoke is easy and my burden is light."

This scripture is a reminder that we can come to God, that we can rest in Jesus. That it is okay to be weak; it is okay to be weary. It is okay to rest in God. My friend, go out there today and be vulnerable and let God be strong. Completely surrender; give up your will. Watch how amazingly God will show up!

Today's Declaration:

"I can do all things through Christ who gives me strength."

Today's Bible Reading:

2 Corinthians 12:1–10

John 15:1–17

Today's Prayer

Thank you, Lord, for calling into mind that it is in my weakness that You are made strong. Please allow me to remember today that I can do nothing apart from You. I give You my weakness today; I give You my challenges today, I give You my questions today. I lay all of these things at Your feet and pray that throughout this day, You will strengthen me, that You will calm me, that You will be with me as Your Word says. Please help me not to rely on my own understanding but to acknowledge You in all of my ways. Father God, I thank you in advance for the day that You are shaping together. I trust You with this day, I trust You with my emotions, I trust You with my life. Thank you for another day in the land of the living. In Jesus's name, I pray. Amen.

Day 12

But my righteous one will live by faith. And I take no pleasure in the one who shrinks back.
— Hebrews 10:38

We have talked about how so much of our negative emotions can be caused by fear. You may be frightened because you don't have a job or because you're sick. In the world, that makes sense, but in our spiritual reality, it goes against everything God wants us to believe about Him. Why can't you trust God? Are you terrified that God won't provide?

Mahatma Gandhi said, "There is nothing that wastes the body like worry. One who has any faith in God should be ashamed to worry about anything whatsoever." Today's scripture tells us that the just man will live by faith. Living is not just a one-time thing; it's ongoing. You don't just walk to the front of the church, accept Jesus Christ as your Lord and savior, and then are done. Living by faith is an ongoing experience. It is more than being baptized as a baby and going to church on holidays. Living by faith must occur every day. We must live a life that shows God that we believe He will do what He says He will do. We must believe that God loves us and that He has a good plan for our lives.

Hebrews 11:6 says that the person who comes to God must believe that God exists and believe that God rewards those who diligently seek Him. There is a reward for faithfulness; part of that reward can be an answer to your prayers! If you don't believe God can answer your prayers, He cannot. You have to believe today that your marriage can be restored. You have to believe today that your body can be healed. You have to believe today that your child will get better! You have to believe today that your dreams can come true. Your belief is the light switch; the power of God is already there, but it is your belief that makes the light shine.

This faith walk is an everyday thing. It is living in faith when you are at church and home, when you are in joy and sorrow. We have to live in faith when we have peace and when we are in despair. It is having faith when you are happy and when you are sad. It is having faith whether the bills are paid or if they are overdue. It is having faith whether you are in the midst of a divorce or are happily married. It is having faith whether you just had a beautiful baby or you just had your third miscarriage. It's having faith in the good times and the bad times. The just man **lives** by faith. Faith is the belief that God is and that He is a rewarder of those who diligently seek Him. The fact that you are on day 12 of reading this book means that you are currently seeking God. He sees it, and He will reward it. Don't stop!

Today's Declaration:

"I live by faith."

Today's Bible Reading:

Hebrews 10:32–39

Hebrews 11:1–6

Today's Prayer

Dear Lord,
   Thank you for Your Word that tells me that the just man lives by faith. Help me to live by faith today. Lord, please remove my fears and replace them with trust. In Jesus's name, I pray. Amen.

Day 13

But we do not belong to those who shrink back and are destroyed, but to those who have faith and are saved. — Hebrews 10:39 (NIV)

Shrinking back is when we allow fear to dominate and control us. It is when we think thoughts like, "I can't do this," or "That job is too big for me." When we have those kinds of thoughts in our minds, we do not allow ourselves to reach our full potential. For example, you may want to say something at a meeting or in a conversation with friends, but you hold back because you are afraid of what others will think. You may decide not to pursue your dreams of getting a master's degree or starting a business because you are scared of failing. So instead, you say half of what you want to say at the meeting, and you go back to school for a certificate instead of the full degree. We allow ourselves to taste a little of God's goodness, but we shrink back from the fullness that is in Him. Our scripture today tells us that if we shrink back, we will be destroyed. When you only reach for a portion of what God has for you, you destroy your dreams and potential to be and have what God wants for you.

Hebrews 10:38 tells us that the righteous person lives by faith. It's scary to talk about the righteous person, right? If we are really honest, who can measure up? It makes it easy to simply infer that Hebrews 10:38 does not apply to you because you are not a righteous person. Who can be righteous? Well, I'm glad you asked! **You** are righteous, and if you currently are not, you surely **can be**. The world has deceived us into believing that a righteous person is someone who does everything right. We think righteous people go to church three times per week, fast every month, pray every day, and never commit sins. Well, my friend, that is a lie from the pit of hell. The Bible tells us in Proverbs 24:16 that the righteous man falls seven times. That means that a righteous or a just man may make seven mistakes and still be righteous. What allows him to continue to be a righteous man? It's because after he sins, he gets back up! After falling seven times, he gets back up and tries again! Being a righteous man or woman does not mean you are perfect (remember that we are created from dust). The righteous person falls then gets back up again. Let me repeat that: they fall, but they get back up again. The righteous man or woman makes mistakes, but they try again. That takes an element of fearlessness and courage. Genesis 15:6 says Abraham believed God, and it was credited to him as righteousness. It is that kind of belief, it is that kind of faith that makes you a righteous person.

When you shrink back or fail to get back up, it not only destroys your mind, but it destroys what God has purposed for your life. When you live small, it does not give glory to God. So, don't shrink back. Live big and strong the way God intended you to live. Use the gift that God has given you in a big way. The best way to tell God thank you for Your gift is to use it. Don't shrink back today! Decide to walk boldly in your Godly purpose!

Today's Declarations:

"I am the righteousness of God. I walk in complete faith today and every day."

"I have courage, and I don't shrink back."

Bible Reading:

Genesis 15:1–21

Today's Prayer

Dear Father God,
   Please help me to live by faith today. Please help me not to shrink back. Father, I depend on You for strength and help and hope. Please empower my mind today. Remind me that You are with me and that with You, nothing is impossible. Help me walk boldly in who You have called me to be with no fear, anxiety, and regrets. Please give me courage for this day. Lord, I love you and praise you. Amen.

Day 14

Faith is taking the first step even when you do not see the entire staircase. — Martin Luther King Jr.

Faith is how I was able to write this book. Faith is what enabled me to survive a miscarriage, a divorce, a blood clot in my brain, and a bankruptcy. Faith is my belief that God is who He says and that He is a rewarder of those who diligently seek Him. (Heb. 11:6). Faith is knowing that although you have difficult circumstances in your life, God is taking all of those things and is working them together for your good (Rom. 8:28). Although it may not always feel like it, and although it may not always look like it, God does have a good plan for your life. Faith believes that Jesus died on a cross and that He rose again in three days so that your sins would be forgiven. Faith reassures me that the thousands of sins I have committed in my life have been cast into a sea of forgetfulness (Mic. 7:19). Faith tells me that if I ask God for forgiveness, my sins are as far away from God as the east is from the west (Ps. 103:12). Faith allows me to understand that God cares more about the intention of my heart than He cares about me attaining material pleasures in this life. God is so concerned that I have a heart that forgives, is grateful, and believes in Him that He is willing to allow me to go through difficulties so that at the end, I get to see His face.

Faith means that you keep going even when you don't know what will happen because you believe in God's providence. Faith is why you have been reading this book every day. Faith is why you can dry those tears away and rest securely in God's loving care for you. Faith is an ongoing trust in God. Faith is obeying Him despite the circumstance or the consequence. Faith is resting your whole weight on God (your heavy load) on His shoulders and not your own. Believe God today! Live by faith and not by sight (2 Cor. 5:7) because he promised to be faithful (Heb. 10:23). God can and will do exceedingly above anything you can ask or even think (Eph. 3:20).

I want you to know that to intertwine your life with God is easy, and His requirements are not heavy to carry (Matt. 11:30). If you don't know Jesus as your personal savior, you can come to Him right now. The Word says that you have to believe in your heart and confess with your mouth the Lord Jesus and that God raised Him from the dead and you shall be saved (Rom. 10:9). So, if you have not done that, I pray that you will do that today. Do it right now. If you already know Jesus as your savior, tell someone else about Jesus today. Share with someone today about the love, joy, and hope you have found. I pray that God will provide you with an opportunity today to share His love with someone. May God bless you and keep you. Have a courageous day!

Today's Declaration:

"I walk by faith, not by sight."

"I confess the Lord Jesus and that God raised Him from the dead."

Today's Bible Reading:

Romans 10

Today's Prayer

Father God,

I will keep going today because I believe in Your providence. Father God, I will not give up today because I believe You are a faithful God who sees me and loves me, and has a good plan for my life. Father God, I love you, and I thank you in advance for working all things together for my good. It is well with my soul because I trust you. Amen.

Day 15

Be still and know that I am God; I will be exalted among the nations; I will be exalted in the earth. — Psalm 46:10

Today happens to be Thanksgiving in my world! I am supposed to be preparing the turkey right now, and I find myself beginning to take on the "Martha spirit." I woke up this morning thinking about all the things I have to do to get my dinner and my house ready for our Thanksgiving guests. Do you recall when we talked about Martha and Mary on our second day? Remember how busy Martha was when Jesus came to her house and how she was concerned that her sister Mary was not helping her? Martha was so worried about cleaning up the house and making sure the food was ready that she went to Jesus and said, "Tell my sister Mary to come and help me." Do you recollect what Jesus said to her? He said, "Martha, Martha, you are worried about many things, but Mary chose the right thing." (Mary decided to sit at Jesus's feet). For those of you with many worries, take a moment to sit at Jesus's feet. I ask you to take a few minutes right now and just think about how Jesus is right there with you. Jesus would love for you to just sit with Him. God loves your company!

Anyone who has adult or teenage children realizes that they spend less time with you as they get older(and if you have young children, believe me, that day will come). Parents of older children, think about how happy you are when your teenage son or daughter wants to hang out with you or when your adult child calls you. God is your Father, and He feels the same way; He loves to spend time with you. Right now, my friend, I want you to think about focusing your thoughts only on the love that Jesus has for you at this moment. I want you to focus your thoughts on the fact that God has it all under control, and He will work all things together for your good (Rom. 8:28).

Remember today that Jesus is enough. God has sent the Holy Spirit to live here on earth with us, and the Holy Spirit is our comforter. As you walk through this day, if you feel anxious or nervous, say a quick prayer. Meditate on your favorite scripture. Do something to connect with God, and then enjoy your day remembering all the things you have to be grateful for. Allow today to be a day of thanksgiving! Try not to be like Martha! Have a great day!

Today's Declarations:

"I am resting in the presence of the Lord."

"My mind is calm, and I am focused on God's love and care for me."

Today's Scripture Reading:

Romans 8:26–37

In your stillness, allow God to direct you further in your Bible reading for today.

Today's Prayer

Dear Lord,

Please help me to be still today. Please help me to cast all my anxiety on You because I know You care for me. Please help me to lean not on my own understanding. Father, I humble myself before You. Please allow Your stillness and Your peace to envelop me. I acknowledge that I can do nothing on my own. I need You for this day. Thank you for life, thank you for hope, thank you for peace, thank you for stillness. Amen.

Day 16

Therefore, since we are surrounded by such a great cloud of witnesses, let us throw off everything that hinders and the sin that so easily entangles. And let us run with perseverance the race marked out for us. — Hebrews 12:1 (NIV)

I need you to know today that many great people of faith have run this race of Christian life. The people we read about in Hebrews have run the race of life with patience and perseverance. How can we do that? How can we keep going amid sorrow, despair, sickness, sadness, and loneliness? Hebrews 12:1 tells us that there are two things we must do. We have to lay aside every weight and every sin that so easily ensnares or entangles us. Today, I don't want to talk about your sin (Hallelujah, because that is none of my business!). Let's talk about those weights, the things that pull us down with heaviness and prevent us from enduring and persevering in this life.

Listen, I don't know what you carry. I don't know if you are carrying the childhood trauma of abuse, I don't know if you're carrying the worry of how your sickness will end, I don't know if you are carrying the worry of how you are going to pay your bills, or the pain of a broken heart. What I do know is that the Word of God tells us we have to take off those weights. If we are running a race, we will never get to the finish line with all these weights attached to us. So, my challenge for you today is to acknowledge the weight and the sin that are holding you down. I ask you to begin to pray about those things. I ask that you start to allow God to remove those things from your heart, soul, and mind. I know this is not an easy process, and it is not something that can be done all in one day. However, there is something helpful in acknowledging they exist. Satan hides in the darkness, in secrets and in places where we don't want to look.

When we acknowledge what has happened to us or the things we have done to hurt others or ourselves, Satan loses his power. Jesus has come so that we can have life and life more abundantly (John 10:10). Satan steals our joy, courage, and ability to live freely and lightly when we carry around old sins, past failures, hurt, and abuse. Today I beg you to talk about it. Find someone you can trust and release it to them. If you don't have anyone to talk to, buy a journal and write about it. Set yourself free. I urge you to consider talking to a therapist, Christian counselor, or even a life coach. There is nothing wrong with getting the help you need to live the life you deserve. My friend, we have a race to run. Don't give up. Lay aside every weight and sin and keep going! You can do it!

Today's Declarations:

"I have great joy ahead of me."

"I will run with patience the race that is set before me."

Today's Scripture Reading:

Hebrews 11:1–40

Hebrews 12:1–3

Today's Prayer

Dear Lord,

Please remove the weight of my heartache, brokenness, and worries from my heart and mind. Lord, I give them all to You. The load is too heavy for me to carry. I surrender it to You. Father, please help me to heal and never to pick up those things again. In Jesus's name, I pray. Amen.

Day 17

Fixing our eyes on Jesus, the pioneer and perfecter of faith. For the joy set before him, he endured the cross, scorning its shame, and sat down at the right hand of the throne of God. Consider him who endured such opposition from sinners, so that you will not grow weary and lose heart. — Hebrews 12:2–3 (NIV)

How do we run with patience the race that is set before us? We should fix our eyes on Jesus. The only way we can run this race of life successfully is if we look to Jesus. We may want to get rid of some bad habits. We may want to stop dwelling in the past. We may not want to carry the baggage of our previous experiences around with us. However, we can do none of those things without Jesus.

I have a friend who believes that God exists, but she struggles with what that means for her. One day, she said to me that people think God is like Santa Claus, that they can just pray and God will give them what they want. Let me stop here. Anyone who has been a Christian for any length of time certainly knows that is not the case! My friend went on to say she does not believe that God should be like Santa Claus, so she does everything by herself. She works hard and does things without asking for God's help. The truth is that because of her hard work and effort, some things in her life are going well. However, I just spoke to her last night, and she feels stuck, is tired, and is burdened. She has run out of patience; she is worn out! She said she just needs life to give her a break. She has done a lot of work on her own. She should be tired! The one thing she has not done is look to Jesus. If we look to Jesus when we are tired and burdened and weary, He will help us.

Matthew 11:28–29 (NIV):

> "Come to me, all you who are weary and burdened, and I will give you rest. Take my yoke upon you and learn from me, for I am gentle and humble in heart, and you will find rest for your souls.

Do you need rest for your soul today? We cannot run the race of life alone. We have to take our burdens and give them to Jesus through prayer and release them. We need to take the weight off our backs so that we can run our race effectively. We can't run our race burdened down with worries. I like the way The Message bible translates Matthew 11:28–29. It says:

"Are you tired? Worn out? Burned out on religion? Come to me. Get away with me, and you'll recover your life. I'll show you how to take a real rest. Walk with me and work with me—watch how I do it. Learn the unforced rhythms of grace. I won't lay anything heavy or ill-fitting on you. Keep company with me, and you'll learn to live freely and lightly."

I know some of you are enduring horrible hardships, and those things will not be easy to get through. But what I beg of you today is to come to Jesus. If you are tired, if you are weary, if you are sick of going to church every Sunday and nothing in your life is changing. I challenge you to change your relationship with Jesus so that He becomes your closest friend. Talk to God, ask Him to help you today, ask Him to help you right now. We have to have a friendship with God that is an ongoing relationship, a never-ending conversation. I promise you He will do just what His Word says if you simply talk to him and lay your cares at his feet each moment of the day. Try it today. Have an ongoing conversation with Him. Ask Him for the big things and the small things. Thank Him throughout the day, and tell Him your thoughts, your dreams. If you want something different, you have to do something different. God is not Santa Claus, but He can certainly be your closest friend. Have a wonderful day!

Today's Declaration:

"I keep my eyes on Jesus, and he takes care of me."

Today's Bible Reading

Matthew 11:28–30

Today's Prayer

Father God, please help me to fix my eyes on you so that I do not grow weary. You are the author and finisher of my life; I trust You with everything. I lean in and depend on You to carry my heavy load. I depend on You for my peace and joy. Father, I know You to be faithful. I love you, and I trust you. In Jesus's name, I pray. Amen.

Day 18

One who has unreliable friends soon comes to ruin, but there is a friend who sticks closer than a brother. — Proverbs 18:24 (NIV)

There have been some hard days in my life, days where I sure did need a friend. I imagine that you have had those days as well. Sometimes it seems as if you are running the race of life completely alone. There are times when even being in the midst of people, you can feel isolated. There are times that the hardships of this life make you feel as if you are the only one in the world who is suffering. Those feelings of loneliness can make it seem impossible to share your experiences with someone else because their lives from the outside seem so good. We think other people cannot understand our struggles. Well, do you know that is a trick of Satan? Satan wants us to feel alone and as if we are the only one who is struggling. Let me assure you today that you are not alone. When you can't go to your friend, you can go to God. When you can't go to your brother or sister, you can go to God. When it is too embarrassing or too hurtful to share with anyone else, you can go to God. On those days when you no longer have the words to describe your anguish or despair, you can go to God. You can cast all your cares on God because he cares for you (1 Pet. 5:7). Not only does God care for you, but he has a good plan for your life. Jeremiah 29:11 tells us that God knows the thoughts and plans he has for your life and that those plans are for good and not for evil, to give you hope and a future. God is a friend who sticks closer than a brother!

We have been talking the past few days about running the race of life, about taking off the anger, the sin, or anything that easily entangles us. We have to run the race God has set for us with endurance and patience. As we look to Jesus and recognize that he endured the cross for us, how can we get weary? Jesus was able to endure the cross because he had a joy set before him. We, too, have a joy set before us, not only in our future life in heaven but in this life on earth as well. King David said, "I would have fainted unless I had believed to see the goodness of God in the land of the living" (Ps. 27:13). Don't faint today! Don't give up today. Keep moving forward, my friend. Keep pressing!

Remember, you have a friend who sticks closer than a brother, and he is right there with you. All you have to do is reach out to him, ask him for help. Talk to him throughout your day. The apostle Paul said to pray without ceasing; that is, to never stop praying throughout your day. Jesus is your friend, and you are not alone. Talk to your friend Jesus.

Today's Declarations:

"I will not faint today."

"Jesus is my friend."

"I will see God's goodness in my life."

Today's Bible Reading:

Psalm 27:1–14

Today's Prayer

Dear Lord,

Thank you for reminding me that I am never alone. Thank you for being my friend; please cover and protect my mind from feelings of loneliness; please remind me today how much You love and care for me. Please help me to keep my focus on You today and not on the circumstances in my life. Help me to wait on You with hope, peace, and joy. I thank you for Your presence. I thank you for Your love. Amen.

Day 19

My heart is not proud, Lord, my eyes are not haughty; I do not concern myself with great matters or things too wonderful for me. — Psalm 131:1 (NIV)

A few days ago, my kids and I were putting up Christmas decorations. My seven-year-old daughter was so happy. You could see the wonder and excitement in her eyes as we went outside to put up the lights. When we were done, she wanted to stay outside to enjoy them. She said she wanted to see how they would sparkle in the dark. After dinner, we decorated the Christmas tree. This time I made my teenage son join us. He helped us and seemed to enjoy it. However, there was a difference in how my daughter decorated the tree compared to how my son and I did. She had a sense of wonder and joy. With each ornament that she hung, she looked at it and asked questions about it. She spoke about how beautiful it was. She took the time to find the perfect place on the tree for each one. I admired her joy. I want that joy. Not to say that my son and I weren't happy because we were. We were listening to one of my favorite Christmas songs by the Temptations ("This Christmas"), and we were enjoying ourselves. However, there was just something different about the way my daughter was experiencing the moment. My son had homework to do, and I'm sure he had other things going on in his mind (as did I). My daughter could be present in the moment and enjoy each part of the experience. What a different way we would be able to view the world if we could do that. What a different experience we could have with life! Psalm 131 (NIV) says:

> My heart is not proud, Lord,
> my eyes are not haughty;
> I do not concern myself with
> great matters
> or things too wonderful for me.
> But I have calmed and quieted myself,
> I am like a weaned child with its mother;
> like a weaned child, I am content.
> Israel, put your hope in the Lord
> both now and forevermore.

My daughter was living this scripture. She was not worried about how the mortgage would get paid; she wasn't concerned about what she would eat for breakfast tomorrow morning. Those things are taken care of; they are taken care of by her parents. Just like the things in our lives that we worry about are taken care of by our Father. So why do we get so caught up in worry? Your heavenly Father knows that you need food and clothes and a roof over your head, and he will provide (Matt. 6:25–31).

Verse 2 of Psalms 131 says, "I have stilled and quieted my soul like a weaned child with its mother." A child is considered weaned when they no longer breastfeed. If you have ever nursed a baby, you know that it can be difficult when you are trying to end it. It's challenging because that child has become accustomed to your breast not only for the nourishment but to provide them with a sense of comfort. At some point, they will come to the place where they are no longer dependent on the breast or the bottle. When a baby is in that place, they have learned to self-soothe. They have learned that their caregiver will provide for them. It may not be a breast or bottle, but they are okay with that. That is what God wants from us. He wants us to quiet our souls even though there are things we want or things we think we need. Can you still and calm yourself, knowing that whatever you need, God will take care of it? There is just something about children. The way they don't worry. The way they can be in the moment and appreciate things. Jesus spoke about that in Matthew 18:1–4 (KJV):

> At the same time came the disciples unto Jesus, saying, who is the greatest in the kingdom of heaven? And Jesus called a little child unto him, and set him in the midst of them, And said, Verily I say unto you, except ye be converted, and become as little children, ye shall not enter into the kingdom of heaven. Whosoever, therefore,

> shall humble himself as this little child, the
> same is greatest in the kingdom of heaven.

The ability to humble yourself, the ability to know that you are not in charge, is essential. Can you say to God, "I humbly submit this to You knowing that You will take care of it," whatever "it" may be? After giving your request to God, can you take your life and still be in the moment and be grateful for it? Can you be thankful for the things that you do have? Can you be thankful for your car even though it makes that terrible noise every time you go over 40 mph? Can you be grateful for your home even though the toilet keeps leaking? Can you be thankful for your job, even if your coworkers get on your last nerve? Today, I need you to focus on the joy and peace that you have in your life. Learn to humble yourself like a weaned child. I invite you to reread Psalm 131, to really read it this time, to be in the moment and ingest what it says.

Still and quiet yourself today. Be still and know that he is God and that he is working things out for your good. Know that God will take care of all your needs. God will do it. Have a great day!

Today's Declaration:

"I am calm and quiet. I am resting in the Lord."

"I am not worried; God is in control."

Today's Bible Reading

Matthew 6:25–34

Today's Prayer

Dear Lord

I am calm; I am quiet; I am resting in You. Thank you for this day. I love you. Amen.

Day 20

Be strong and courageous and do the work. Do not be afraid or discouraged, for the LORD God, my God is with you. — 1 Chronicles 28:20 (NIV)

King David wanted to build a temple to the Lord; however, the Lord told him he was not the man to do it. The Lord promised him that his son Solomon would build it. In 1 Chronicles 28:20, King David is speaking to Solomon about building the temple. God ordained Solomon to build it, it was part of God's plan, but David told Solomon that he had to do the work. It's the same with you. God has a plan for your life, but you will have to be strong, and you will have to do the work. Hallelujah! The purpose that God has given you, the dream that God has given you, will require you to do the work.

I don't know what your work is. I don't know what your dream is. I don't know the purpose God has for you, but I believe that God does have a purpose and a plan for your life. I need you to dig deep! I need you to be strong and courageous. I need you to be bold, and I need you to do the work. Do the work, even if it makes you feel foolish. Do the work, even if it makes you feel like you don't know what you're doing. Do the work and be strong. I have learned that when you are doing God's work and following the Holy Spirit's promptings, you will sometimes have to do things that make you feel uncomfortable, things that don't make any sense, and things that require you to be bold and courageous.

There have been so many times in my life when I have felt just ridiculous and foolish, but I felt this prompting from the Holy Spirit, so I had to do it anyway. An example of that is when I was asked to preach at a local church. It was the first time I had preached outside of my home church. I was nervous, but it went well. The following Sunday morning when I woke up, I felt a prompting in my spirit to go back to the church again. So, I said (in my whiny voice), "Lord, why do I have to go back? That's gonna make me look like a crazy stalker, and I don't wanna do it." I got out of bed and went to my church, and then after service, I went back to the church I preached at the previous Sunday. When I arrived, it was toward the end of the service, so I sat at the back of the church. When the service ended, I went and stood next to the pastor. The pastor told me I had been on her mind and she wanted to talk to me about something but would do it at a later time. I said okay, but before I left, I told her I felt that God had told me to come to the service today and that I would keep coming every Sunday until she felt ready to talk. Now let me tell you, I don't know where those words came from, and after saying them, I felt like a crazy stalker! However, after I said that, she said, "I want you to come every fifth Sunday, and I want you to preach at this church." Wow!

Having that assignment has been such a blessing to my life, especially since I had only been a licensed minister for a month when this happened! It may not have happened if I didn't follow the guidance of the Holy Spirit. I felt silly, but sometimes that's part of this process, pressing forward even if you don't feel like it, going out and trying to reach your goals even if they seem impossible. Pressing, pressing, pressing so that you can achieve the purpose and the plan that God has for your life.

Today's Declarations:

"I am strong."

"I am courageous."

"I will do the work."

Today's Bible Reading:

1 Chronicles 28:1–21

Today's Prayer

Dear Lord,

Thank you for another day in the land of the living; please help me to be strong, please help me to be courageous. Please help me to do the work. Lord, I ask that You give me courage and grace as I walk through this day, help me do Your will, and manifest the plan You have for my life. In Jesus's name, I pray. Amen.

Day 21

The secret of change is to focus all your energy not on fighting the old, but on building the new. — Socrates

There is no fear in love. But perfect love drives out fear. — 1 John 4:18 (NIV)

My friend, the new that you are building is love. When you focus on loving God and loving yourself, the fear will dissipate. Remember that fear is not from God. Do that thing that you fear; that's when fear loses its power. When you walk in love, Satan loses his power. Fear cannot function in love. When you love God enough to do what He tells you, you conquer fear. When you love yourself enough to follow your dreams, you conquer fear. When you finally realize that God loves you so much that He is always protecting you, that love from God will conquer your fear.

Sure, you will have moments of doubt and fear associated with change and doing something new. As humans, we all experience this from time to time. Allow God's love for you and your love for yourself to overcome those temporary fears. Fear's purpose is to stop you from moving forward. Love's purpose is to help you grow. Growth does not always feel good. Sometimes it is downright awful. But nothing lives or flourishes without growth. For a seed to grow, it must disintegrate into the dirt to become the flower or the vegetable it was meant to be. Disintegration is often painful but necessary for the new thing to take place. You see your breaking is a prerequisite for your next level. I ask you today to surrender.

For 21 days, we have talked about fear, we have spoken of faith, we have talked about love. My prayer for you is to continue this journey. Now that you have gotten into the habit of spending time with God every day, keep it going. As of the day of this writing, the Fear Not video blog that I post on my Facebook page has reached day 224. I encourage you to continue your journey there if God leads you in that direction.

I pray that God continues to cover, bless, and keep you in Jesus's name.

Today's declaration:

"God loves me with his perfect love."

"I am free to accomplish God's purpose for my life!"

Today's Bible Reading

John 14:1–31

Today's Prayer

Dear Lord,

Thank you for loving me with Your perfect love. Thank you for guiding me to this book. Thank you for the past 21days. Please help me to put into practice the things that I have learned. Please bring them to my mind when I need them most. Help me to focus all my energy on You, help me build the new in my life. Please release joy and peace in every area of my life and help me walk in boldness to the things You have called me to do. Please help me lay aside every weight and every fear that is holding me back from becoming the person You have created me to be. Father God, I love you and I praise you. In Jesus's name, I pray. Amen